QUICK
GUIDE
TO WINE

QUICK GUIDE TO WINE

A Compact Primer

ROBERT JAY MISCH

DRAWINGS BY MAC SHEPARD

DOUBLEDAY & COMPANY, INC.
GARDEN CITY, NEW YORK

This is for Janet,

My dear wife, who had the original idea for a short, terse book for those who want to know "just enough" about wine, without pedantry or tedium. I hope I have done what she wanted—for her and for them!

JxxxxB

CONTENTS

viii

INTRODUCTION

I remember very well the end of Prohibition in the United States.
I came over shortly after the Noble Experiment had been laid to rest. As President of the British Wine and Food Societies, I was anxious to form a chapter in New York. With the help of such dedicated wine people who remembered back as Frederick Wildman, Julian Street, Richardson Wright, Henry Taft, Sophie Kerr, Jeanne Owen—to name a few—the Society was duly launched and a young chap named Robert Jay Misch became its first Secretary. I am telling no tales out of school when I say that he didn't know why. Bob knew mighty little about wine in those days except that it came in bottles. As a young "man about town," his had been a homemade gin era!

Bob became my good friend; he still is, despite the disparity in years. He was avid to learn; I was avid to teach him. We got along famously. He had two loves: the greater, Janet, the girl who became his wife and my dear friend too. The other love was wine. He has been loyal to both all his life, as two lovely daughters, Kathy and Mary, and this book, testify.

It is indeed a "slim volume" for it was not the author's intention to produce an encyclopedic dissertation on wine. Rather, it is Bob's attempt to acquaint others with "just enough" about wines, their service, and their enjoyment.

André L. Simon

PRESIDENT, WINE AND FOOD SOCIETIES

FOREWORD

A little knowledge is *not* a dangerous thing, in wine!

There are plenty of meritorious volumes on the subject, usually ponderous tomes that tell you more than you care to know, or can possibly remember. The result is either ennui, fright, or belligerence —either "Oh! who cares"; "Heavens, if there's all that to learn, I give up now"; or "Phew! I'm sticking to scotch and martinis."

But, if you're going to drink wine (and I think you should because it adds a very pleasant new dimension to living), then you might as well know a little about it—enough to enjoy wines *more,* and to enjoy *more* of them.

I feel rather strongly on the subject because I know from my own experience that wine can really *make* a dinner—the simplest or the most elaborate. It can soothe the savage breast and mellow the frosty heart, and unlike stronger drink, it seems to bring out the affable rather than the animal, and produce euphoria instead of amnesia.

I take it that, at the moment, you don't care at all whether the '28s ever did soften up, or that Romanée-Conti escaped the phylloxera epidemic, or that chaptalizing is permitted in certain vineyard areas —and so on and so on and so on.

All I intend to do in this slim volume is to suggest a few bench marks on wines and their service; disabuse the uninitiate of some of the clichés, pronouncements, and dogmatisms of the pundits and wine snobs; and perhaps help in casting off the chains (of the sommelier, in this case) from your own considered judgments.

Then you can proclaim your new-found freedom from can't and cant! Your own personal taste should be the final determinant of what you drink. We are not a nation with a wine-drinking tradition. We are not born to the purple—or the white, or rosé. Hence, it seems to me, quite sensible and proper to "read up" a little on the subject. Information cannot come by osmosis. Unlike the French, brought up with wine, we sometimes become a bit precious as we learn more; sometimes doctrinaire. Don't! Wine isn't a holy mystique —it's just a very pleasant liquid of infinite variety that adds to the pleasures of the table. Don't be afraid to drink what you like—and say so. If a sweet wine pleases you, don't necessarily get on the "dry" bandwagon—until you mean it! You probably will, one day, as your taste becomes more perceptive and cultivated.

One word of caution! Beware *too much* freedom! To revolt against the Lucullans, it is not necessary to go whole hog the other way. The wine boor is no better or worse than the wine bore. While lightning won't strike if you serve a rich, red wine with your brook trout, or a light, white one with your roast, it would be a surprise if you preferred this departure from the usual. And just because glassware and temperature and vintage and such need not be followed to the letter, it doesn't mean that a dubious 97-cent special, served in a nicked coffee mug, is just the thing either. Laissez-faire with common sense—that's the right way, as it is in most everything. If this little book starts someone on the road to Romanée, and helps give some pleasure along the way, it will have served a splendid purpose.

R.J.M.

QUICK
GUIDE
TO WINE

THE
CATEGORIES
OF WINE

It is said that one could girdle the earth at the equator with different wines (as usual "laid end to end") and do it twice without a duplicate! Consequently I never can quite understand anyone who says "I don't like wine." There are so many wines, of all degrees of sweetness, dryness, redness, whiteness, thickness, thinness, mellowness, sharpness, timidness, aggressiveness, lightness, headiness, that it would seem likely some would please the most critical palate.

Generally speaking, there are four major categories—table wines; fortified wines, or wines to which brandy has been added to increase strength; apéritif or flavored wines; and sparkling wines.

Table Wines

These are, or should be, simply the juice of certain grapes, fermented (the process which turns the sugar in the juice into

I

alcohol), clarified, aged for varying periods in tanks or barrels, and then bottled. That's all. These wines are usually relatively low in alcohol, from 9° to 14°. By their very definition, they are served at "table" along with food.

Table wine is white, red, or pink, and all shades in between. It is primarily a question of how long the skins of the red or black grapes are allowed to stay in the vat when the wine is being made. All the coloring matter is in the skin of the grape. Leave the skins in long enough—you have red wine. Take them out sooner—rosé or pink wine. Don't leave them in at all—white wine. Some grapes are, of course, green or, as they are called, "white." There is no skin pigmentation. These grapes produce white wines only.

Fortified or Dessert Wines

This is probably an unfortunate descriptive word—"fortified." It simply means that after the normal fermentation of the grape sugar into alcohol has been completed, a strength of 14°, give or take a degree, is the maximum. To go beyond this, brandy is added to bring these wines around the 20° mark. Incidentally, when brandy is added *during* fermentation, fermentation ceases, some sugar is left unconverted, and you have a sweet drink like Port or Muscatel. If you add the brandy *after* fermentation is completed, you *can* have a dry drink, such as the dry Sherries.

SHERRY, named after the city of Jerez in Spain, is the most famous of this great family of wines. It is made primarily from the Palomino grape. The transcendent characteristic of Sherry is a certain "nuttiness" of flavor. The genesis of Sherry is the *Solera* system. This means that great casks, or butts as they are called in Spain, containing Sherries of different ages, but always of the same type, are stacked in a vast "organ" of wine—the bottom casks containing the oldest wines. The blender draws off what he needs from his various tiers, to make the blend he wants, as a conductor leads his orchestra. After the blender

has used what he needs, the oldest tier is refilled from that next above, and so on, new wine being added at the top. In this way, a perpetual supply of aging wines is at his disposal, but obviously no "vintage" can apply as each cask holds wines of many years.

The most mysterious thing about Sherry is that often the grower never knows the *type* he will get when he presses his grapes. Only while aging does each cask take on its particular characteristics!

The principal types of Sherry are:

Fino, Manzanilla, Vino de Pasto—dry; serve cold.

Amontillado—moderately dry; chill.

Amoroso, Oloroso, and "Brown"—rich, sweet; serve at room temperature, though now often served "on the rocks."

Dry Sherry might come, more properly, under the heading of apéritif wine, that served *before* a meal. The sweeter Sherries are dessert or "in-between-meal" wines. All of this is very glib and very pat; it just doesn't happen to be entirely true! Bristol Cream of Harvey's is a sweet Oloroso Sherry, yet it is the largest seller in the U.S.A. Obviously, that's not because it's drunk "between meals"—few wines are, these days. No, it's drunk *before,* but "on the rocks," the new order of the day. Famous Dry Sack of Williams & Humbert is a huge seller— not *dry* really, yet also used as an apéritif, and also chilled or iced. Sweet American sherries and other sweet wines are often given the same ice treatment! The old "order" changeth, giving place to new.

PORTS come from Oporto in Portugal. They, like the Sherries, are primarily blended wines and come in various gradations of sweetness. None are really dry.

The major varieties are:

Ruby—blends of young-bottled wines, fruity, rich red in color, sweet.

Tawny—usually older wine, blended and matured in wood, brownish red, not so sweet.

White—yes, there are some, often denigrated as a "woman's drink."

Vintage and Crusted—rare and costly. Vintage ports are wines of the grapes of one year. Bottled early, they are allowed to mature for many years because these Ports do improve in the bottle. They "crust" or throw much sediment. Handle with care.

MADEIRA is another of the fortified dessert wines. At one time it was a great favorite of the early colonists. George Washington, it is said, was a "two bottle a day man." Madeiras deserve greater popularity than they currently enjoy. They can be very pleasant drunk "on the rocks" (yes, the ice mania has struck Madeira, too), or with a rich soup, or in place of Port at the end of a meal. The types (all named for their grapes of origin, except "Rainwater") are:

Sercial—reasonably dry, a fine appetizer; serve chilled.

Bual (or Boal) and Malmsey—sweet and rich, for dessert or with a biscuit, between meals; serve at room temperature.

"Rainwater"—This great Madeira was produced in Savannah from imported casks of other Madeiras. The secret of its preparation has been lost, although prototypes are still marketed under the name. Quite dry; serve chilled.

Verdelho—a dry Madeira from the almost extinct Verdelho grape; akin to Sercial.

Other dessert wines are MALAGA from Spain, MARSALA from Sicily, and MUSCATEL from Spain or Portugal.

TOKAY, from Hungary, is an historic wine, one known to

have great medicinal properties. I have been hard put whether to list it here or under table wines. The main types are:

Szamorodni—dry, could be quite properly served as a table wine; chill.

Aszu—sweet, contains overripe grapes. A dessert or "between-meals" wine; chill or not.

Eszencia—rare and almost impossible to obtain. I mention it only because some consider this to be the greatest of all wines. It is produced in infinitesimal quantities, drop by drop, by the simple pressure of trays of grapes, stacked one on top of the other (no squeezing). The apocryphal story is that Emperor Franz Josef of Austria-Hungary annually sent Queen Victoria of England a dozen bottles of "Eszencia" for each year of her age—indeed, a "princely gift." (Who else could have afforded 972 bottles, when she was eighty-one, at $7.00 a bottle?)

Apéritif Wines

The next group of wines are the apéritif or "flavored" ones. The best known is VERMOUTH. Vermouth is simply an infusion of wines with various herbs, roots, barks, etc.—the combination all highly secret and known to the maker alone. Vermouth can be dry or sweet. Usually the dry is known as French and the sweet as Italian. These are misnomers as the larger firms, no matter where located, usually make both types. The U.S.A. is a large producer of Vermouths. The Dubonnets, St. Raphaëls, Lillets, Byrrhs (there are dozens of other brand names) are also essentially flavored wines, and their formulae are the secret of their makers. They are drunk straight or are used as mixers with other ingredients. All Vermouths and their derivatives and all apéritifs are served cold as cold can be.

A new group of *flavored* wines has recently appeared on the U.S. horizon—the flavored "special" wines of large U.S. producers. "White Satin," "Thunderbird," etc.—who hasn't heard of these?

Sparkling Wines

Of course, the one that first comes to mind is CHAMPAGNE. Champagne is more than a wine—it's a way of life! People have actually been known to ask, "Should I serve wine or Champagne tonight?" as if Champagne wasn't wine but a thing apart. Champagne is wine which has not had its second fermentation completed—hence the bubbles in the bottle. Champagne is difficult to make, costly to make, time-consuming to make, and taxed outlandishly by Uncle Sam.

The classic Champagne is made only by the *Méthode Champenoise*, the contribution to our joy of a French cellarmaster-monk, Dom Perignon, at the end of the seventeenth century. His was basically a method of making practical the fermentation of wine, a second time, in the bottle. The process was known, but his experimentation with corks and bottles made the process possible. Besides the true *Méthode Champenoise*, there is a cheaper *Charmat,* or bulk, process, where the wine is treated in pressurized vats. (Look at the label; it tells you—by law.)

The Champagnes of France are, of course, the original ones— and the only true ones, according to the French. In France, the name Champagne is applied to the wines made in the demarcated area of Champagne around Reims and Épernay. Almost all are white, a few pink, none red.

Other countries have produced what they call "Champagne." Spain recently lost a test case attempting to send Spanish "Champagne" to England. The shipment was stopped. It was a sparkling wine all right, and made by the *Champenoise* process. "But," said the English courts, "it isn't Champagne."

Probably the next most important sparkling wine (there really is no "next") is Sparkling Burgundy. This is primarily an export to us. Americans love it. Such big shippers as Chauvenet, B & G, Calvet, and Chanson do a big business in red bubbly.

Germany calls her sparkling wines Sekt. Other countries and other areas of France itself produce "Sparkling this-or-that"; viz. Sparkling Anjou, Sparkling Vouvray, Sparkling Saumur. Italy calls hers Asti Spumante. But in a decision going back to 1904, the U.S.A. declared that a sparkling wine of Champagne characteristics *could* be called Champagne if it was qualified by the additional words "California" or "New York State" or "Ohio," in large type, on the label. The French have never accepted this decision, as you can well imagine, and don't like it a bit. Actually, the United States does make some very fine "Champagnes," call them what you will.

A note about so-called "vintage" Champagnes. All Champagnes are blends of wines, sometimes of several years. Each producer mixes wines into a *Cuvée,* a word for *blend.* If it is an exceptional year, however, then the vintner dates or "vintages" his bottles. You pay more, and usually (but not always) it's worth it!

"Sparkling," as such, means truly bubbly—as in Champagne. But often a wine has a slight prickle. You can taste it on your tongue. This effervescence is too slight to be called "sparkling." The French call it *pétillant* and the Germans, *spritzig.* It is not at all uncommon for wines to ferment slightly in the bottle and to have a slight effervescence. This is not a "bad mark." It is often sought after.

RED WINES

The Red Burgundies of France

These include some of the greatest wines in the world. What makes a Burgundy—or for that matter, any wine—great? This is a subject that could be argued for days—and has been! Let us just say it is a matter of *balance* between acidity (or tartness) and sweetness; *color* or "robe"; *bouquet* or "nose" —the smell of the wine; the wine's *trueness to the type* of grape from which it is made; and the wine's ability to *improve with aging* in the bottle. To these add *breed* and *body*. "Breed" is a subtle thing—hard to describe. You sense it when it's there— as you do in people. Perhaps you might call it a "wellborn" quality. "Body" means *substance,* or the opposite of watery or thin.

Let us suppose that you are planning a dinner centering around a nice roast beef or steak. Usually, either suggests a red table wine. At least they do to me. (At the end of this book, you will find charts listing what goes well with what, and approximately how much it costs.) You could have a Burgundy, a Red Bordeaux, a Rhône, an Italian wine, a Spanish wine, a wine from one of the smaller producing countries (Hungary, Portugal, etc.), or an American counterpart. For this chapter, let us decide on a Burgundy.

Burgundies are wonderfully full, big wines. They have an ease about them on first acquaintance, and a charm. The Burgundy family runs the gamut from the princes of the blood to nephews of the brother-in-law.

All of the great wines of Burgundy are produced along what is called the Côte d'Or, or Golden Slope, a relatively small area of France, south and east of Paris, centering around the charming provincial city of Beaune. In turn, the Côte d'Or is divided into the northerly Côte de Nuits (more famous for reds) and the southerly Côte de Beaune (more famous for whites but with a few *great* reds). Beaune is roughly, but not quite, the divider.

The wines of Burgundy differ from those of Bordeaux (to be discussed in the next chapter) in that the vineyards have never been classified or evaluated by an official committee of experts. But the wine lovers of the world have long made their judgments, and these are as binding as *any* law! Another difference between these two—the greatest wine areas in France—is that Burgundy vineyards are seldom owned by a single proprietor. A few, and sometimes more than forty proprietors (Clos de Vougeot) own bits and pieces. The famous Hospices de Beaune, the great hospital of the Côte d'Or, owns acreage in dozens of vineyards, the gifts of grateful patients. The owners do not all harvest or market individually; often they pool their output, and make and sell jointly. Thank heaven for that, or there

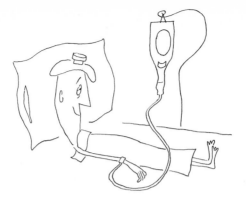

would be no end to the names. The nomenclature is hard enough as it is. My rule of thumb for you is to get to know some of the *shippers*. Their names are your guarantee: Latour, Drouhin, Laguiche, Moreau, Leflaive, Sichel, Jadot, Ropiteau, and the great houses of Chanson, Chauvenet, Calvet, B & G— there are many more—are names to buy by. Some deal only in esoteric greats, for the very knowledgeable—others, like the last four, have their own wholly owned vineyards but primarily buy, blend, bottle, etc. as *négociants,* and prefer to ship good wine in some volume, and with greater consistency.

The grapes of Burgundy are the Pinots, noble but light-bearing grapes: Pinot Noir is for the red ones and Pinot Chardonnay is for the whites. The Gamay is not "noble"; it is a heavy-bearing grape that makes Beaujolais and a few of the lesser wines, but never the true *noble*men. The great Beaujolais area, planted to this grape, is not along the Côte d'Or, but *is* in the Burgundy area.

There are a succession of communes or parishes along the Côte d'Or, running from Fixin in the north to Santenay in the south. Between these are the great vineyards of Burgundy. Farther south lie not only the aforementioned vineyards of Beaujolais but also Mâconnais. These are classified as Burgundies, but are not nearly so great. To the north and west is the world-famous acreage of Chablis—Burgundy, but with special characteristics. All of these lands together produce only about one third as much wine as Bordeaux, and of this, only a small percentage, about 20 per cent, is entitled to bear a particular estate or vineyard name.

A vineyard name and/or the legend *"Mis du Domaine,"* *"Mis en Bouteille au Domaine,"* *"Mis en Bouteille par le Propriétaire,"* or *"Mise à la Propriété"* mean "Estate Bottled." All great Burgundies are *Appellation Controlée*—that simply means a jealously guarded name, indicating the point of origin of the wine.

Township, parish, or commune wines can be good but they are not the so-called "greats." Le Chambertin, for instance, is a "great" vineyard, whereas Gévrey is simply the town in which it is located. Because of the preëminence of the vineyard Chambertin, lesser wines of Gévrey are often called Gévrey-Chambertin. Where Chambertin is a *Grand Cru,* "Great Growth," Gévrey-Chambertin would be only "Premier or First Growth." Believe me, many's the Gévrey I've had (and other commune wines) that was little short of the most patrician. Another example: Vosne-Romanée is just a parish or district, the name Romanée being added to Vosne because it is unquestionably the best-known name in red Burgundies. Wines by the name Vosne-Romanée may be fine but are usually not in a class with such vineyard wines *within* the area as La Romanée, La Tâche, Richebourg, and of course, Romanée-Conti, the *incomparable.*

Here might be the place to clear up another puzzler; namely Romanée-Conti vs. the *Domaine* de la Romanée-Conti. Romanée-Conti is considered by many to be the greatest red wine of Burgundy, if not in the world. Romanée-Conti is *one* of the vineyards of the Domaine of Romanée-Conti; so are La Tâche, parts of Grands Échézeaux and Richebourg, etc. These magnificent wines bear their own names as well as that of the Domaine. Every bottle of these wines is numbered, every cork branded, every grape babied and tended as no others in the land. The price tags will quickly convince you!

You'll see in the chart section that I list such great, great *Grand Crus* as La Tâche, Chambertin, Les Grands Échézeaux, Richebourg, etc., selling for $6.00 to $15.00 a bottle. For lesser wines, I list good "First Growths" of Vosne-Romanée, Gévrey-Chambertin, etc., for $3.50 to $6.00. And I also list some inexpensive Beaujolais. Most Beaujolais are blended of wines from anywhere in the Beaujolais district. But a few come from towns entitled to special *Appellation Controlée*. Some are Morgon, Brouilly, Fleurie, Moulin-à-Vent, Juliénas. They won't

cost more than $1.75 to $3.00, and are usually worth a few cents more than those just called Beaujolais. (*Note:* Don't overdo Beaujolais! There are *other* quite inexpensive red wines. There is a danger of late; too many people are becoming Beaujolais "Johnny One Notes." There just isn't all that *decent* Beaujolais made, for one thing, and variety is the spice of wine, as well as of life, for another.)

Contrary to usual red Burgundy procedure, Beaujolais is often served chilled. It can be very young. Beaujolais is a major *carafe* wine of France; that is, wine served right from the wood, in a pitcher or carafe.

I repeat this because it is so important. There are so many "cooks" making Burgundy, even from the same vineyard, the name of the producer or shipper (or importer) on the bottle is most important. In Bordeaux, Château Margaux is Château Margaux, no matter who ships it or who imports it. There is only one owner, one maker, one wine. But in Burgundies, a bottle of Corton or of Pommard of one house may be quite different from another. Learn to distinguish and know some shippers' names whose wines you've enjoyed. There is no short cut to this. You simply have to learn some; meantime, rely on your storekeeper or your hotel or restaurant to guide you.

The Red Bordeaux of France

Directly southwest from Burgundy, toward the Atlantic, lies the Bordeaux area of France—probably the most famous vineyard acreage in the world. Here is the land of the Châteaux, the world of Clarets. A Claret is simply a red Bordeaux, from the French *Clairet,* meaning a light red wine (red they are but light, not always!).

There are hundreds of Châteaux. Don't try to distinguish

them all. As you've learned to identify Picasso and Manet, distinguish Mozart from Beethoven, you'll learn to know a percentage of them in time—and a percentage is enough!

First, what is meant by a "Château"? Everyone knows a Château is a French castle or manor house. But in wine, a Château name is used to identify the wine of the grapes grown in the demarcated area around or near said Château, and made into wine there. All Châteaux wines bear the *Appellation Controlée,* or "controlled" name.

Clarets come from four great areas (like counties, you might say, in the same state): Médoc, Graves, Pomerol, St. Émilion. (Sauternes is the fifth Bordeaux division of major importance, but all Sauternes are white. A few Graves and a Médoc or two are white. They will be discussed later). The Médoc is further divided into communes such as Pauillac, St. Julien, Margaux, St. Estèphe—but suffice to know there are fine Châteaux in all these areas and also fine regional wines called by communal names: Margaux (without the Château prefix), St. Émilion, etc., or simply Bordeaux, or Bordeaux Supérieur. These are not estate-grown or bottled. They are blends but often can be delicious, and usually sell at a much lower price.

Clarets, in general, are longer-lived, and take longer to mature than the Burgundies. Some are fragrant, delicate, as in the Médoc—some, like the St. Émilions, can be very robust.

The great Clarets of song and story, First Growths (*crus* is the word used in France to differentiate between gradations of wines; it translates as "growth," for no very good reason), are Châteaux Latour, Lafite Rothschild, Haut-Brion, Margaux— and today, Mouton Rothschild. They were so classified by a panel of experts in 1855, and pretty well still live up to their laurels in 1966. (Mouton Rothschild then was a "Second Growth," but today is accepted as certainly the peer of the others.) Only the wines of the Médoc and Sauternes were *officially* classified a century ago. Generations of winebibbers differentiated the others, unofficially, until 1953 (for Graves) and 1955 (for St. Émilion); Pomerol still remains to be done.

Here is the official listing of 1855 but, for heaven's sake, don't take it *too* literally. Châteaux can change their rungs on the ladder of excellence thanks to the skill of the vintner, propitious sun or rainfall, proper viticulture in one Domaine as against another, or even Lady Luck. Don't become a slave to charts or listings, or anything else—in wine. Few of us are that palate-trained anyhow, as to be able to distinguish a Second from a Fourth, a Third from a Fifth. The list is printed solely in the interest of your being able to see what Châteaux are "in." Half the fun is "discovering" for yourself.

Classification of 1855
Médoc Wines

First Growths
Château Lafite
  (now Lafite Rothschild)
Château Margaux
Château Latour
Château Haut-Brion

Second Growths
Château Mouton
  (now Mouton Rothschild)
Château Rausan-Ségla
Château Rauzan-Gassies
Château Léoville-Las Cases
Château Léoville-Poyferré
Château Léoville-Barton
Château Durfort-Vivens
Château Gruaud-Larose
Château Lascombes
Château Brane-Cantenac
Château Pichon-Longueville,
  Baron de Pichon
Château Pichon-Longueville,
  Comtesse de Lalande
Château Ducru-Beaucaillou
Château Cos d'Estournel
Château Montrose

Third Growths
Château Kirwan

Château d'Issan
Château Lagrange
Château Langoa-Barton
Château Giscours
Château Malescot-Saint-
  Exupéry
Château Boyd-Cantenac
Château Cantenac-Brown
Château Palmer
Château La Lagune
Château Desmirail
Château Calon-Ségur
Château Ferrière
Château Marquis d'Alesme-
  Becker

Fourth Growths
Château Saint-Pierre
Château Talbot
Château Branaire-Duluc
  (now Branaire-Ducru)
Château Duhart-Milon
Château Pouget
Château La Tour-Carnet
Château Rochet
Château Beychevelle
Château Le Prieuré
  (now Prieuré-Lichine)
Château Marquis de Terme

Fifth Growths
Château Pontet-Canet
Château Batailley
Château Grand-Puy-Lacoste
Château Grand-Puy-Ducasse
Château Lynch-Bages
Château Lynch-Moussas
Château Dauzac
Château Mouton d'Armailhacq
  (now Mouton-Baron Philippe)

Château Le Tertre
Château Haut-Bages-Libéral
Château Pédesclaux
Château Belgrave
Château Camensac
Château Cos-Labory
Château Clerc-Milon-Mondon
Château Croizet-Bages
Château Cantemerle

Sauternes and Barsac

First Superior Growth
Château d'Yquem

First Growths
Château La Tour Blanche
Château Lafaurie-Peyraguey
Clos Haut-Peyraguey
Château Rayne-Vigneau
Château Suduiraut
Château Coutet
Château Climens
Château Guiraud
Château Rieussec
Château Rabaud-Promis
Château Sigalas-Rabaud

Second Growths
Château de Myrat
Château Doisy-Daëne
Château Doisy-Védrines
Château d'Arche
Château Filhot
Château Broustet
Château Nairac
Château Caillou
Château Suau
Château de Malle
Château Romer
Château Lamothe

Note: In the Graves listing of 1953, below, Haut-Brion appears again—duplicating its appearance in the 1855 listing. That is because this one Graves vineyard had an importance all its

own, even a century ago, and was taken out of context and
listed with the Médocs.)

Classification of 1953

Graves

Classified Red Wines
Château Bouscaut
Château Carbonnieux
Domaine de Chevalier
Château Fieuzal
Château Haut-Bailly
Château Haut-Brion
Château La Mission-Haut-
   Brion
Château La Tour-Haut-Brion
Château Latour-Martillac
Château Malartic-Lagravière
Château Olivier
Château Pape Clément
Château Smith-Haut-Lafitte

Classified White Wines
Château Bouscaut
Château Carbonnieux
Domaine de Chevalier
Château Couhins
Château Kressmann La Tour
Château Laville-Haut-Brion
Château Malartic-Lagravière
Château Olivier

Classification of 1955

St. Émilion

First Classified Great Growths
Château Ausone
Château Cheval-Blanc
Château Beauséjour-Lagarosse
Château Beauséjour-Fagouet
Château Belair
Château Canon

Château Clos Fourtet
Château Figeac
Château La Gaffelière-Naudes
Château Magdelaine
Château Pavie
Château Trottevieille

Great Classified Growths
Château L'Angélus
Château L'Arrosée
Château Balestard la
  Tonnelle
Château Bellevue
Château Bergat
Château Cadet-Bon
Château Cadet Piola
Château Canon La Gaffelière
Château Cap de Mourlin
Château Chapelle Madeleine
Château Chauvin
Château Corbin
Château Corbin-Michotte
Château Coutet
Château Croque-Michotte
Château Curé Bon
Château Fonplégade
Château Fonroque
Château Franc-Mayne
Château Grand-Barrail-
  Lamarzelle Figeac
Château Grand-Corbin-
  Despagne
Château Grand-Corbin-
  Pecresse
Château Grand-Mayne
Château Grand-Pontet
Château Grandes Murailles
Château Guadet Saint Julien

Château Jean Faure
Château Clos des Jacobins
Château La Carte
Château La Clotte
Château La Couspaude
Château La Dominique
Château La Cluzière
Château Clos La Madeleine
Château Larcis Ducasse
Château Lamarzelle
Château Larmande
Château Laroze
Château Lasserre
Château La Tour du Pin
  Figeac Belivier
Château La Tour du Pin
  Figeac à Moueix
Château La Tour-Figeac
Château Le Chatelet
Château Le Couvent
Château Le Prieuré
  (Saint Émilion)
Château Mauvezin
Château Moulin du Cadet
Château Pavie-Decesse
Château Pavie-Macquin
Château Pavillon Cadet
Château Petit-Faurie-de-
  Souchard
Château Ripeau
Château Sansonnet

Château Saint-Georges-Côte-
Pavie
Château Clos Saint Martin
Château Soutard
Château Tertre Daugay

Château Trimoulet
Château Trois Moulins
Château Troplong Mondot
Château Villemaurine
Château Yon-Figeac

And certainly when the Pomerol area is codified, as very soon it must be, Château Pétrus will come to the top, like cream, for the cream it certainly is!

Most Clarets grow old gracefully, hence older vintages *are* available because producers, middlemen, and sellers do not market fine Bordeaux too young. They *are* jumping the gun a little of late and producing wines that will mature younger. Five years is about the youngest at which *good* Clarets are drunk; then fifteen, twenty or more is not uncommon for the best. It is difficult to generalize because wines of different years have different characteristics and will mature at different rates. The '59s seem to have matured very rapidly, while '55s have not. Some say wines of '28 never have!

23

The storage of wine too has something to do with the rapidity of maturing. A Claret in the cool, cool cellars of its Château will not mature as rapidly as the same wine kept in an apartment house closet or in the superheated garret of a country home (perish forbid!).

Label-reading is an art in itself. It cannot be learned overnight. But remember, all labels do not lie, although a few may weasel! Wine men are not charlatans. It may be that you do not understand what the label is saying. Here are a few warnings of what to guard against in reading labels, not that a masquerading wine is necessarily going to poison you—but you *should* get what you pay for.

Appellation Controlée, in France, is your "sterling" mark of authenticity of *origin*—and nothing else. Without it, *Grand Vin* or any other designation, means nothing.

Mis en bouteille au château means "made and bottled at the château" *and no where else. Mis dans mes caves* or *Mis en bouteilles en Bordeaux* does *not* mean estate bottling.

Pretty pictures mean nothing. Some of the greatest wines come in the simplest bottles.

"Château" is generally applied only to wines of Bordeaux. A few, very few, other vineyards use the term—a few in the Loire, even one or two in Burgundy—but for a rule of thumb, Château means a Bordeaux estate. (And a few, a very few, Châteaux do not use this "Château" designation— "Domaine" or even "Clos" may be employed.)

And perhaps this might be as good a place as any to point out another thing. All French wine—in fact, all wine of *any* country—isn't necessarily great. Much isn't even bottled. Most wine is drunk *en carafe*—that is, drawn from a barrel in the restaurant or host's cellar, and poured into a pitcher or tankard or other container. It is young. It is the drink of the countryside. I suggest you try these *vins ordinaire,* red or white, when traveling. Also you'll encounter certain *vins de pays,* the local or regional wines of the district. These are usually bottled, but seldom shipped, being deemed either too inexpensive, or else "poor travelers." Some wines simply cannot stand being sent from one place to another. Their delicate chemistry is upset. They do not taste the same as they did at home. So try these wines in their own bailiwicks. It's all part of the fun.

The Red Rhônes of France

The wines of the Rhône, grown farthest south in France, along the great river, have the color of red-purple velvet. They are deservedly popular with some; not well enough known to others. Highly seasoned food will especially appreciate a Rhône, a wine able to stand up to it.

There is a great deal of Rhône wine produced. Only a little of it is exceptional. Côte Rôtie, which means "roasted slope," is probably the best. Hermitage (its vineyards produce both red and white wines) can be very good indeed. The most famous of all, Châteauneuf-du-Pape, is named after the vineyards owned by the Popes when they left Rome and lived in Avignon. There is a lot of it. It has become a sort of Beaujolais of the Rhône. When it is good, it is very, very good, and when it is . . . well, you know the rest.

Rhône reds are made by blending the juices of many varieties of grape. There are few if any Châteaux or Estates as such. A shipper's name—one like Chapoutier—is something to look for—or a fine importer, like Wildman. Don't drink Rhônes too old —three to seven years is enough—except for Côte Rôtie which takes longer than other Rhônes to smooth out. Rhônes can be very good values. Use them where you would a lesser Burgundy.

The Italian Red Wines

Italian wines do not pretend to compete with the *greatest* wines of France. However, these "greats" represent only 8 to 10 per cent of total French production. Italy does compete with the regionals, the lesser Châteaux, lesser Burgundies including Beaujolais, and the Rhônes. The government is now playing a major role in a carefully planned rebirth and policing of the industry. That's why Italian wines today afford such excellent values.

There is great variety in Italian wines. Italy is no longer known only for Chianti, in its familiar straw *fiasco*. Matter of fact, the best Chiantis usually come without straw. These have greater bottle age, being bottled young and allowed to mature in the bottle. The straw-covered Chianti is more likely to have been kept in a vat until needed, then bottled in a hurry and shipped. Chianti *can* be a very good wine. To be sure of getting the Chianti *Classico,* look for the "cockerel" on the neck label. Another mark of excellence is the *Putto,* or little "angel," on the neck label.

Some other red Italian wines worth trying are Barolo (a fine robust wine of real substance), Bardolino, Barbera, Grignolino, Nebbiolo, Valpolicella (deservedly popular), and Gattinara (excellent).

You needn't worry too much about vintage in Italy. It doesn't mean a lot. In Italy, equable climate keeps most vintages uniformly good. The best producers are now more interested in blending for quality, uniformity, and *continuity*. All too often in the past, the Italian wine you liked and ordered one day was very different on reorder. Gradually, this situation is being corrected, thanks to governmental insistence and greater care and skill in the Italian vineyards.

A Few Other Reds to Try

Spain's red Riojas (there are some white) can be very pleasant table wines, and well worth trying. They resemble regional Clarets.

Portugal's "little" red wines like Dão or Colares are often good (Mateus is a good name).

Yugoslavia's Merlot, Dingač, Blatina, Cabernet, Plavac are excellent, if you can find them, as are Hungary's Egri Bikavér ("Bull's Blood") and Kadarka.

Greece's wines are mostly white, but red Naoussa is a delicious table wine that you should seek out. Red, sweet Mavrodaphne is a famous rich *dessert* wine.

Switzerland's Dôle is worth a go; also Turkey's Trakya and Buzbag.

The American Red Wines

The great Ignoble Experiment called Prohibition, which happily was terminated in 1933, set American wines back vastly. Progress in quality production ceased. Fine vines were plowed under. Skilled vintners went into Insurance or Wall Street. It is to the everlasting credit of the dedicated men—and yes, women—in the wine industry, both East and West, that they were able to "get with it" so quickly and so successfully, in the three decades since repeal. Now American wines can well hold their own, without chauvinism or the need for extravagant claims, with the wines of the Old World. This is as it should be because America has been blessed with some of the finest grape acreage, soil and climate being what they are, to be found anywhere.

American wines have a character and qualities peculiarly their own. The grapes (in California, that is, which represents 85 to 90 per cent of our production) are from European vines, the family of grapes known as Vitis Vinifera. Very sensibly the producers of some of the best wines of California are now using the names of the *variety* of grape from which the wine is made—hence, their designation—"varietals." For instance, the grape that makes red Burgundy is the Pinot Noir; to make Bordeaux, it's primarily the Cabernet Sauvignon; for Beaujolais, the Gamay. You buy American varietals by these very same names: Pinot Noir or Cabernet Sauvignon or Gamay. These wines are offered under the labels of many American vintners.

There are plenty of other wines from California, of course, aside from varietals. Some producers still use European names such as California "Chablis" or California "Burgundy." These are the "generic" or semi-"generic" wines, which have their own characteristics, and often very good too. They do *not* have to contain 51 per cent of a varietal grape. Other wines are known by their "brand names" just the same as "proprietary" brands in anything. These latter are special wines, the product of large and reputable companies, which market under their own exclusive names and labels. They seek to develop and blend specialty wines which will always be uniform, which the consumer will like and come back for, year after year.

Napa, Sonoma, Livermore, and Santa Clara circling San Francisco are deemed the best table wine growing areas of California, but specially developed new hot-climate hybrids and the regularly "hot" grapes of Italy and Spain do very well farther south. Primarily the difference between the California and European producer is that the latter usually offers only one kind of wine, while in California, one producer will offer a dozen. He feels his varied topography and acreage permits the growing of various kinds of grapes. In France, he would grow only one, or a very few—sometimes by choice, but in the great vineyard areas, by law. Another thing to remember is that some California wineries are small and their production limited. Their wines will not always be available readily, but are sought out, much the same as the limited-production "name" wines of Europe.

Are California wines better, or worse, or the same as their European counterparts? Why not try them yourself and see? Your steak or roast would do well paired off with either. This I *will* say: they may not taste *exactly* the same because a grape, after all, is a pump—not a thing unto itself! In Burgundy, a Pinot Noir grapevine pumps what's in *that* soil and drinks in *that* sun and *that* rainfall. In California it does the same—but six thousand miles away, with all the attendant variations. Is a French Canadian an exact replica of a Frenchman *or* a Canadian? Obviously not. Result—two somewhat different taste sensations with subtle likenesses. You decide which you like. Probably the answer will be both, for variety, and not snobbery, tests the true mettle of the wine lover.

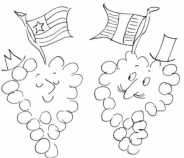

Among the American varietals, the names you should know are these:

Cabernet Sauvignon—this from the grape that makes the great red Bordeaux of France. It is probably California's most successful wine. It can be delicious, made by one of many dedicated growers (see charts) and I suggest that it improves vastly with a little bottle age. (Buy two cases and put one away a year or two. You'll see.)

Pinot Noir—the counterpart of red Burgundy. Bottle age plays its part here too. A sturdy wine.

Gamay—a pleasant, light wine from the Beaujolais grape.

Zinfandel—a peculiarly Californian product. It is unknown in Europe, though the vine is a Vinifera, a European grape. Light in body, heavier when from southern California.

Barbera, Grignolino—these "Italianate" wines can also be had from California. (Also "Chianti"—not a "varietal.")

Also seek out, and try out, some of the proprietary labels; that is, wines that bear the names given to them by their makers, and are exclusive with that maker.

Incidentally, gallon and half-gallon jugs, as used for certain wines, merit your attention. After all, what are magnums and jeroboams but oversized containers? Jug wine *can* be very good and a very good buy. Experiment to find those you like.

There are also red wines made in the East, in New York State and Ohio, primarily. (Most eastern wines are Champagnes or still white wines.) They are made from native American grapes, hybridized, and are not from European vines or grapes, although some crossbreeding is now taking place. The American is an entirely different family of grapes called Vitis Labrusca. You will find bottles called New York State Burgundy, New York State Claret, under such established names as Taylor, Great Western, Gold Seal, and Widmer. Meier's of Ohio is a fine maker. Some of these wines have the characteristics of the American grape—what the oenologists (wine scientists) call "foxy" or grapey. That doesn't mean you won't like them, but if you're expecting a counterpart of their European namesake, they're not. However, in late years, hybridizing with Vinifera stock has much reduced the "foxiness" previously associated with eastern wine. Whether you think this is an improvement or not is up to you. I rather think it is, but sometimes the unblushing Labrusca can make a wine that need not blush either. It is—as always—a matter of taste.

American wines can be marvelous values, yet so often you have to press to get them because of (*a*) wine snobbery, (*b*) wine ignorance on the part of the storekeeper or restaurant, (*c*) a certain self-interest—American wines often cost less and hence the profit is less per bottle. For *goodness'* sake, seek them out—insist—demand.

WHITE
WINES

With "white" provender—fish, seafood, certain poultry dishes, and the like—experience suggests a white wine. There is a vast array to choose from. Again, let us go to the five great areas mentioned before for the Reds: Burgundy, Bordeaux, Rhône, Italy, and the U.S.A.—but for white wines we shall add the Loire, Alsace, Germany (and yes, Switzerland, Austria, Hungary, Yugoslavia, Chile, South Africa, and Australia).

The White Burgundies of France

White Burgundies are superb. They are dry, full, robust. Le Montrachet, queen of white Burgundies, is pretty generally conceded to be the greatest white wine of France. It's certainly about its most expensive! Corton-Charlemagne isn't far behind. Or you can settle for one of Le Montrachet's hyphenated neighbors such as Bâtard-Montrachet and Chevalier-Montrachet. You get a *bit* less but you pay a *lot* less!

One of the white Burgundies you *do* know is Chablis, but, fair warning, all that passes for Chablis, shouldn't! It's a lovely wine when right, with that unique, "flinty" taste. Here again, the shipper's name is *so* important. Get to know some by trial and error. Another help, sometimes, is to ask for a Chablis that is classified and not just "Chablis," such as these *Grand Crus:* Chablis-Vaudésir, Chablis-Grenouilles, Chablis-Valmur, or Chablis-Les Clos.

Meursault, another fine white Burgundy, can be truly great, especially Meursault Les Perrières, Les Genevrières, or La Goutte d'Or; delicate and lovely.

And let us not forget the ever-popular Pouilly-Fuissé from the Mâconnais area of Burgundy to the south, near Beaujolais. This is another catchall name. It can be fine. (Wines never become popular for no reason.) But it can also harbor, under the Fuissé label, wines that should not disgrace the name. Here again is where shipper and importer's name must help in your selection. Ask your storekeeper, restaurateur, or the best judges of all, your own taste buds.

The White Bordeaux of France

White Bordeaux are many and varied. Let us start with world-renowned Sauternes, a white Bordeaux. Because of the fame of the name, often they are the first wines tried by the neophyte. At some risk I'm going to stand up and say that a Sauternes is *not* the wine to serve with your chicken or turkey or through the meal. Too sweet! (Note the final "s" on Sauterne*s*. This is traditional whether there is one Sauternes or several. The U.S.A. uses no extra "s," usually.)

There are no "dry" Sauternes among the imported ones. A dry finish or aftertaste, yes, but there really is no *dry* Sauternes from France. (From California there are *drier* ones.) Sauternes, especially Château d'Yquem, are lovely in their place—with dessert, or even between meals with a sweet biscuit. As in the red wines of the Médoc, in 1855 an official codification of Sauternes was made. Château d'Yquem, and only Château d'Yquem, was yclept *Premier Cru Supérieur*.

Other top white Bordeaux are Châteaux Climens, Coutet, Rayne-Vigneau, and especially La Tour Blanche. These are all *Premiers Crus*. They are all superb. They are all sweet. They cost much less than d'Yquem. Some are from the commune of Sauternes, others from the communes of Bommes, Preignac, and Barsac. Barsac you will often see under its own regional name. It is always sweet.

There are also some dry*ish* white Bordeaux, from the Graves area. Many of the Châteaux of the Graves make red *and* white —even the great Château Haut-Brion makes a *blanc*. Château Margaux in the Médoc offers a white Pavillon Blanc. Château Olivier is a well-known dry Graves, as are Châteaux Carbonnieux and Haut-Bailly, among others.

The White Wines of the Loire

Vouvray is probably the best known of the Loire wines. It is not dry. It is usually a little *pétillant,* or prickly on the tongue. (There is a completely *sparkling* Vouvray, also.) Vouvray is marvelous on a hot day, served at a roadside stand along the Loire. I have never thought it tasted the same over here.

Muscadet, a modest enough little white, is light, delicious, and *so* inexpensive. Brittany is proud because Muscadet is her only *controllé* wine.

Pouilly-Fumé (not to be confused with Pouilly-Fuissé of the Mâcon in Burgundy), sometimes known as Blanc Fumé de

Pouilly, is a distinctive wine—with a distinctive "earthy" taste. It is most pleasant. Ladoucette's Château du Nozet is top-drawer Pouilly-Fumé; there are others, of course.

Sancerre is another Loire wine, somewhat like Fumé, and worth trying. Ditto Quincy, this harder to find over here, but available, and a very good value.

Two other famous Loire names are Anjou and Saumur. Anjou is the biggest Loire district and Saumur is part of it. Anjou and Saumur wines can be dry or sweet, and some are sparkling. The English seem to know Anjou and Saumur wines much better than we do. Pity.

The White Wines of the Rhône

While it is true that most Rhône wines are red, there are a few whites worth mentioning.

Hermitage Blanc is exceptionally good, especially the one boasting the lovely name Chante-Alouette. La Chapelle is another. (Hermitage Blanc, different from most whites, takes two or three years to mature and be ready to drink.) Château

Grillet is considered the finest white Rhône, but don't bother looking! The whole vineyard is 2.7 acres; little wine ever leaves the vineyard.

White Rhônes are difficult to describe. Not as bone dry as a Burgundy, they are not sweet, are very full-bodied and have a strong and delightful bouquet.

The Jura and Provence are two other wine-producing areas with bottled wines of some note. Arbois is another name you may encounter, and the Provençal Bandol and Cassis wines are sometimes, though not often, found away from home base.

The White Wines of Alsace

It is almost tautological to say "white" for Alsatian wines—*all* the ones we see are white. They are pretty much an extension of the wines of Germany (Alsace has been German, you will remember) and are presented in the same tall, thin bottles. Riesling is the pre-eminent Alsatian, and mighty good it can be. Other wines from Alsace are the Traminer, Gewürztraminer (a "spicy" Traminer), and Sylvaner—perhaps not quite so dry

as Riesling, but ever so refreshing of a summer's day. Growing farther south than the German Rhines and Moselles, Alsatian vintage years are not quite so important, and few if any estate bottlings and special bottlings are to be found. Splendid values —the wines of Alsace. Hugel, Willm, Dopff are good shippers.

The White Wines of Germany

The white wines of Germany are *as a group* probably the greatest white wines of the world. They consist of the richer Rhines (or Hocks as they're called in England), and the lighter Moselles. *Tip:* Rhines come in brown glass bottles; Moselles in green, and they are *all* in that thin, tall bottle (except for ones called Steinwein which come in a squatty *Bocksbeutel.*) Don't try to learn all the German names—they're jawbreakers. But to purchase German wines sensibly, some knowledge is necessary. In the morass of words on the labels you will see some new terms to decipher:

Auslese—wine from selected grapes.

Spätlese—wine from late-picked, very ripe grapes.

Beerenauslese and *Trockenbeerenauslese*—wine from overripe grapes, almost raisin-like.

(All of the above terms indicate grapes which have been allowed to contract the *pourriture noble,* or noble rot, by being left long on the vine. They develop this mysterious and *beneficial* grape malady which makes for a lovely sweetness and a fabulous "bouquet." Great Sauternes achieve their luscious sweetness because of the same microorganisms in the decaying grape.)

Cabinet or *Kabinett-wein*—the proprietor's own wine, the best he can make.

Originalabfüllung—means the same as "Estate Bottled" and *"Mis en Bouteilles au Château"* in France.

Bernkastel, Piesport, etc.—the towns in which a vineyard is located. This is followed by the vineyard name: viz.: Bernkastel is the town, and Bernkasteler Doktor the famous vineyard in the town; Piesport is the town—Piesporter Goldtröpfchen is a vineyard of Piesport.

Fass or Fuder—means cask or case, each is followed by a number, pinpointing the particular wine in the warehouse or cellar.

Naturwein, Naturrein—natural, no sugar added. There are plenty of other "no sugar added" terms such as *echt, rein, ungezuckerter,* as sugaring is a point of great importance in Germany where all too often the grape juice or "must" does not contain enough of its own sugar to make a successful wine.

Rhine Wines—The charts at the end will tell you the names of some Rhines in various classes. A few to look for: Schloss Vollrads, Marcobrunner, Schloss Johannisberg (all fruity, but not so sweet); Niersteiner, Oppenheimer, Forster Jesuitengarten (sweeter). Liebfraumilch—so well known to Americans—is a generic term that encompasses a multitude of sins, as well as wines. The name applies to *any* wine grown in the entire Rheinhessen—the area from Bingen, Mainz, to the city of Worms, and almost to Mannheim. That's why one so-called Liebfraumilch will cost $1.29 and another $2.99. Why not try some of the less well-known wine names? (Exceptions in Liebfraumilch: "Blue Nun" from Sichel; "Crown of Crowns" from Langenbach; "Hanns Christof" from Deinhard; "Liebfraumilch Glockenspiel" from Kayser; "Liebfraumilch Rheinsonne" from Steigenberger.) The shipper and the importer are your protection. Kayser, Deinhard, Sichel, Steigenberger, Langenbach, and Hallgarten are some excellent names to remember.

Moselles—The production of Moselles is relatively small. The wines are lighter, dryer. Berncasteler Doktor is by far the most famous, most expensive, and scarcest. Have it, if your ship comes in. Seek out Piesporter Goldtröpfchen, Wehlener Sonnenuhr, or Graacher Himmelreich, if your ship is still at sea! Moselblümchen—the Moselle's counterpart of Liebfraumilch, —is a catchall generic name for often very dubious wines of the whole area.

One other thing—drink German wines young—one, two, three, four years; never more than ten, except for the *Spätlese*, or rich, rich *Beeren* and *Trockenbeerenauslese* wines, which can have a very long life—some up to fifty years, so rich, fruity, and balanced in acid and sugar are these noblemen.

And don't think you're alone on names, or the complications of the messages on German labels. They have always been the bane of the Rhineland.

The White Wines of
Italy, Switzerland, Austria, Hungary
Greece, Yugoslavia, Spain, Portugal, Chile
South Africa, Australia, Turkey

Italy has a plethora of white wines. The good ones are good indeed. One of the best is Verdicchio di Jesi, from the lovely hill town, Castelli di Jesi. It is light, dry; comes in a unique Mae West-shaped bottle you'll never mistake.

Est Est Est is famous, but only its name and its legend please me. It seems a bishop sent his servant on a journey to search out the best wine at the inns along the way. He was to write "Est" on the wall where the wine was good. He did so but suddenly came upon a wine so great that he wrote "Est! Est!! Est!!!" When the good bishop arrived, he drank so much he expired right on the spot! I find it too sweet.

Orvieto is justly famous. There are two kinds: the dry, or the fruity sweet. Ask for the one you mean. Capri is a pleasant dry white, but by all odds, Soave! A *good* Soave is delicious—bone dry, so refreshing, so inexpensive. Frascati, from the village of the same name in the Alban Hills south of Rome, is popular and becoming more so; I'm not sure I know why.

Switzerland—Everyone seems to know Neuchâtel. I prefer Dézalay or Fendant (the varietal wine from the Fendant grape). These wines are light, inexpensive—not unlike Alsatians.

Austria also suffers from being best known for one white wine, Gumpoldskirchner. It is fruity, fragrant. I prefer a Kremser or a Loibner Kaiserwein, from the Wachau district. Often the names of the grapes, as in California—Riesling, Gewürztraminer—are used for other Austrian wines.

(*Heurige* is *not* a wine but a name given to new wine and the incredibly gay celebrations that accompany its advent every vintage season. A green branch hangs out to indicate "the new wine is here," and the Viennese flock to the *stube,* laden with sausage and bread. It's great fun—until the next morning!)

Hungary's whites are exceptionally good, especially from around Lake Balatón. Badacsonyi is excellent (there are several of these, ranging from dry to medium); also Debröi and

Somlyöi, these sometimes with additional appendage or hyphenated names. Of course, Tokay is *the* great wine of Hungary. (Discussed before.)

In *Greece,* to preserve wines in the old days, they placed them in pine barrels or resinated them; that is, they flavored them with pitch. They still do. It's an acquired taste. I haven't acquired it! There are plenty of good, unresinated wines, such as St. Helena, Pallini, Cave Minos, etc., to try. Many of the islands make wine. Byron loved the wine of Samos. The volcanic island of Santorin is a producer of good local wine, as is Corfu. Probably the finest grape area of Greece is not far from Athens; Achaia Klaus, best-known Greek producer, has large holdings there. (Metaxa, known the world over, is not a wine but a heady brandy.)

Yugoslavian wines can be very good. Not too many are available here, but you're going to be seeing them more and more because Yugoslavia is endeavoring to go into all manner of export. You'll have to take what you can find, but do try them. Zilavka is a lovely, dry, Riesling-like wine; also recommended: GRK, Opolo, and Rizling.

Spain makes a white Rioja. The Marqués de Riscal and the Marqués de Murrieta are good shippers. I much prefer Montilla, a sherry-like, dry wine, unfortified, from the district next to Jerez. Serve it before a meal as an apéritif, or with the meal as a table wine, which it is.

Portugal makes a vast variety of very pleasant white wines, the majority of which never leave the country; Vinho Verde is the best known.

Chilean white wines are really dry and inexpensive. Undur-raga is a "best buy." It comes in the *Bocksbeutel* (a squatty flask) traditional for the German Steinweins.

South Africa and *Australia* are also large producers—but most goes to England or stays at home. Remember Constantia among the Africans; Yolumba is an Australian white.

Turkey's little-known Kulüp Sarabi, from around Ankara, is lovely, if you're a good prospector and can find it; also try Trakya and Barbaros.

The American White Wines

In America, we have white counterparts of European wines, as we have red ones. Some of these also employ the "varietal" names of the grapes from which they are made: Riesling, after the grapes of the Rhine and Moselle; Sylvaner and Traminer, after the grapes of Alsace; Semillon and Sauvignon, from the grapes of the Graves and Sauternes; the Chenin Blanc from those of the Loire; Pinot Chardonnay and Pinot Blanc correspond to the white grapes of Burgundy. (There is also a *Grey* Riesling—not a true Riesling, and an Emerald Riesling, a recently produced hybrid.)

Many of these are delightful wines, but different in some respects from their European siblings. Try them. A few makers, like Wente, Concannon, specialize in whites. California was justly proud recently, when one of Wente's Pinot Blancs was awarded the accolade of excellence by an anonymous Guide Michelin man. (See list of other good vintners, under California Reds.) Drink all these wines young (one to three years). Bottle age doesn't mean much to them, as it does to the reds. Matter of fact, after two to four years, many whites tend to become yellow and *maderisé*—a polite way of saying not palatable.

We even have an "unknown" white—that is, from a grape unknown in Europe today. It's the "Green Hungarian," pleasant, light, quite dry, named for the Hungarian Count Haraszthy whose grapevine cuttings, brought from Europe in the mid-nineteenth century, launched California's entire wine industry. (Lucky thing, too. These European vines, planted here, were found to have an immunity to the dreaded phylloxera, or plant louse, which threatened to wipe out all of Europe's vineyards in the '80s. Immune root stock from America was thereupon sent overseas and saved the day—and the grapes!)

In the whites, too, there are some wines that use European nomenclature—the generics: viz., California Chablis, Sauterne (without an "s")—and there are also many proprietary labels. Most are blends of wines, some of which have natural flavors added. They maintain a continuity, uniformity, and a distinctive taste. Try some—they have millions of enthusiastic devotees.

The Finger Lakes of New York, Ohio, a bit of Pennsylvania, Maryland, and even the Hudson River Valley produce *eastern* white wines. Their greatest success is in sparkling wines, but there are also some interesting still whites as well. Delawares, Ionas, Niagaras are grape types which Widmer makes

into very pleasant wines called Lake Delaware, Lake Iona, Lake Niagara, etc. Philip Wagner, of the Boordy Vineyards in Maryland, and Charles Fournier, of Gold Seal, upstate New York, have probably done the most for eastern grapes in their hybridizing and experimentation. The best-known eastern names are Taylor, Great Western, Widmer, and Meier's in Ohio. Charles Fournier is making some excellent white wines.

Ports, Sherries, Angelicas (18–20 per cent alcohol) are also made in New York State.

Champagnes

Even to the most unknowing, to people who never drink wines, the names of Krug, Moët & Chandon (including their world-famous Dom Pérignon *cuvée*), Perrier-Jouët, Mumm,

Irroy, Veuve Clicquot, Mercier, Laurent-Perrier, Ayala, Taittinger, Bollinger, Roederer, Lanson, Ruinart, Pommery & Greno, or Heidsieck (both Charles and Piper-) are household words. They are the great French Champagnes.

The reason for the bubbles in Champagne is that the wine in the bottle is undergoing a second fermentation, which is captured by the cork and wire, and hence the "stars" are held in for you to drink! Champagne is expensive because it's costly to make, in time and in labor. For instance, every bottle of Champagne must be first fitted with a temporary cork. It must be stored, slanting downward for long months; every bottle must be given a slight turn two or three times a week so that the impurities, produced by the continuing fermentation, can filter down and settle around the cork. Then the neck of the bottle is immersed in a brine solution and frozen. The cork, and a pellet of ice around it, are literally shot out (taking the impurities along). The gap left at the top of the bottle is then given a dose of sugar syrup and Champagne, depending on the sweetness desired for the finished bottle. It is recorked, wired, and sealed, and stored for a year or more before shipping. And on top of this, Uncle Sam puts his tax—about four to six times what he charges for still wines! Now do you see why Champagne costs so much when made by this process? (The bulk, or *Charmat*, process for producing bubbles in huge pressurized tanks is, of course, much cheaper—and generally so is the wine.)

Champagnes can be of various orders of sweetness:

Brut—the driest (the *brut* called "English Market" by some producers is often drier than the *brut* for the U.S.A.). In California, the driest is called *"Natur."* Serve any time, with or between meals. Champagne is the *one* "all-purpose" wine!

Extra Dry—dry, but not quite as dry as *Brut*. Treat same as *Brut*. It is for many who don't *really* like so dry a wine as *Brut,* and admit it!

Demi Sec—fairly sweet. Dessert wine.

Sec or *Doux*—very sweet. Seldom made since the Tsars.

There is also some pink Champagne made, the tint coming from the black grape skins. And there are *blanc de blancs* Champagnes (Taittinger is the best-known French one, and Almadén, the American). These are made entirely from white grapes, without the usual admixture of black grape wine. Ay and Cramant are regional all-whites.

American Champagnes

Perfectly delightful California Champagnes are being made. Almadén, Masson, Korbel, Weibel, Kornell, Beaulieu, Cresta Blanca come immediately to mind as making bottle-fermented or transfer wines. Christian Brothers, Léjon, Italian Swiss, Roma, Maitre D', and now Gallo, make *Charmat*-process champagnes. New York State also produces Champagnes, somewhat fruitier since the grapes are native; Taylor, Great Western, and Gold Seal are the well-known names.

ROSÉ
WINES

A Rosé is simply a wine in which the grape skins have been allowed to remain long enough in the vat, after crushing, for the color of their skins to tint the wine pink. In its place, Rosé can be very good, but that doesn't mean *every* place, or as a compromise between red and white. It isn't. Rosé is a wine unto itself.

Rosés can be pleasant with shellfish, with roast veal or pork, baked ham, even a barbecued chicken or steak, on a hot day when a heavier red wine would be out of place.

Tavel (from the Rhône) was the first, is the most famous. Château d'Aqueria claims to be the only *Premier Grand Cru* of Tavel. Sichel's "Pavillon de la Rose" is another lovely Tavel.

We get other French pinks from Arbois and Anjou. Château Ste. Roseline is a famous one from Provence.

California makes very good Rosés—Grenache Rosé of Almadén is justly famous, as are Wente's Livermore Rosé, Ingle-

nook's Navalle Rosé, Martini's Mountain Gamay Rosé; also Krug, Cresta Blanca, Paul Masson, Beaulieu, Buena Vista, Gallo, Christian Brothers, Roma, Guild, Italian Swiss and a host of others feature pleasant Rosés. Paul Masson offers an American "Crackling Rosé"—truly a "sonnet from the Portuguese!"

Italy's Rosés from the Lake Garda area are most pleasant. Even Germany and Alsace have gotten into the act lately. And Lancers, a "Crackling Rosé" from Portugal, is vastly popular. Another of the same type from Portugal is Mateus, also in the fancy, stone crock. These fancy containers probably do more to sell the wine than the rather soda-pop-y wine itself!

VINTAGE

This subject is "fraught with interest"—and danger. Mild-mannered, quiet men tend to froth at the mouth when the subject is mentioned. Personally, I feel vintage occupies too much time and attention—too much poring over charts, talking numbers, and drinking years rather than wine.

Vintage means the synthesis of weather and physical conditions of a specific growing season. I'd be the last one to call vintage in northern *European* wines unimportant. There are good years and poor years, and in-between years, and you'll pay accordingly. But don't become a slave to charts. In every poor year some good wines are made. And I'm afraid the opposite is also true! After all, you can't blame Mother Nature for everything! How the grapes are grown and selected and processed by the vintner also determines the quality of a wine.

Italy, Spain, and Portugal do not have the weather variations that France and Germany do. Hence, their vintage marks are of much less moment. In fact, I wouldn't pay too much attention. Often they're given vintage marks simply to please the American penchant for them.

In California, there is a chasm between the vintage and the non-vintage adherents. Though the cliché that "every year is a vintage year in California" is out, it *can* be said that, compared to the variability of northern European growing seasons, California's years seldom show *marked* variations. The largest producers are mostly opposed to vintage labeling, preferring to blend various wines for uniformity and continuity of type. If they use a vintage identification, then, by law, every drop must be of that year. This, for the most part, they refuse to do (although some are now beginning to "vintage"). But many of the smaller producers of Napa, Sonoma, Santa Clara, and Livermore usually support vintage, and point out what they consider differences in the wines made in this year over that year, in a cloudy year, in a sunny year, to prove their point. Slight differences *do* exist from year to year. Whether they are due to weather factors, or are primarily the result of differences in bottle age, is open to argument—and what argument! As far as I am concerned, "you pays your money and you takes your choice!"

THE SERVING
OF WINES

The French use the word *présentation* to describe the way food is presented. The Chinese go even further—fussing about texture contrasts, sweets vs. sours, color combinations. Two chefs may make two dishes exactly the same way, but what a difference the presentation makes! The same can be true of wine. The simplest, least expensive, most unassuming wine can be presented properly.

That doesn't mean elaborate fancy cut glass decanters. It doesn't necessarily mean baskets for the wines to lie in and to be served from—though these are sometimes appropriate for really old bottles. It does mean simply service, generous glasses, and pouring with a little style, preferably by the host himself. It's a pleasant custom for the man of the house to dispense the wine, no matter how many servants there may be. And when he does, he shows the label to each guest or tells the assemblage the wine they are drinking. This isn't ostentation. It's just courtesy. This business of "Guess what?" is stupid, I think.

Smoking? You'll have to be your own arbiter. I rather dislike being schoolmastered myself, and I hate to order my guests about. However, it *is* true that wine and smoke don't mix. If you're serving just an unexceptional *vin ordinaire,* don't fuss. If, however, you've brought out a really fine wine, it should be shown deference. Why not pointedly leave cigarettes and ash trays off the table, and if asked, "May I smoke?" say, "Would you mind not, until after the wine?"

Water glasses? Leave them off too. This American way of watering down every meal is more a habit than a necessity. Serve wine or wines, that's enough liquid.

Glasses

Here, I *am* a fuss, but only in one department—size. By all that's holy, get rid of those itsy-bitsy wine glasses, even if they're made of crystal or cut glass, have been in the family for generations, or were given to you by dear Aunt Maude. For one thing, a wine glass should be large enough to allow the bouquet or fragrance of the wine to collect in the top of the glass. That

means you will fill the glass only half full. With a small glass, you've only a thimbleful of wine or, more than likely, a slopped over and stained tablecloth.

Should wine glasses ever be tinted? One of the beauties of wine is its color—the ruby and garnet reds, the topaz and straw-colored whites. Why hide them behind opaque walls, or tinted ones?

Old Rhine wine glasses were once tinted green, amber, red, to hide the flecks and motes floating in improperly clarified wine. This is no longer necessary. German vintners have learned to produce impeccable wines. These tall glasses, though, do lend a charm to a well-set table—use your own judgment.

And a proper wine glass *should* have a stem. An 8 or 9 oz. tulip, available at any store, can be your all-purpose glass. If later, you want to splurge on a wider, larger, hold-more glass for red wines, by all means, do so. Two sizes of glasses for the service of two wines is very elegant. Have the glasses of the same make or design though, unless you have some special treasures that are both serviceable *and* conversation pieces.

Table Wines Are Alive

Wines are subject to change—*table* wines, that is. If they weren't, they wouldn't be good wines. They are young, they mature, they grow old in the bottle. Pasteurized wines (wines cooked to a high heat) and fortified wines (wines that have been brought up to higher proof by the addition of brandy or other spirits) are inert and will not change in the bottle. What went in comes out. When you hear someone say "My father had this Sherry (or this whiskey) before Prohibition," it means absolutely nothing. If it was good then, it still is; if not, it won't be now. But if he says, "My father had this *wine*," that's another matter. Depending on type, it could be transcendent, drinkable, or foul.

But don't be alarmed; wines do not need all the pampering you hear about. Just a little normal regard will serve you, and them, well.

Keep 'em Quiet

First, don't treat wines like tenpins. Don't roll them around more than you have to. Some people feel the proper place for wine is the shelf in the coat closet. Every time a hat is taken out to wear, the bottles roll over. Every time the hat is put back, they roll over the other way. Wine should be kept as quiet and untouched as possible. That means try not to call George at the office and ask him to "bring a couple of bottles home for dinner—the Dibbles are coming." He'll bring it all right, all shook up. That doesn't do you, or the wine, justice. Wines (especially reds) hate jiggling. But why not keep a supply on hand and serve wine *regularly,* not just on "special occasions"?

Storage

Table wines with corks should be kept lying on their sides; table wines with patent screw caps can stand up. Nothing esoteric about that. It simply keeps the corks immersed in wine, hence wet, hence swollen, hence airtight. The entrance of air into wine leads to *Götterdammerung,* the twilight of the Gods! Of course, you *could* stand wine straight up for weeks, even months, and probably nothing drastic would happen—but why chance it?

Too much heat or too much cold are as bad for wine as for

other living things. So, don't keep wine next to the radiator or the steam pipe, or standing in the sunlight, and don't let it freeze. In between these extremes, don't worry so much. Few have cellars these days, or temperature-controlled wine bins. Just normal temperatures will have to do. I've lost mighty few bottles even in an unair-conditioned apartment in a steamy July. (Heat does speed up the maturing process, though.) Try to find a dark closet, or a piece of one, for your best bottles.

Stores, these days, are featuring all manner of wine racks— from simple affairs of wire for a few dollars for the cellar, to handsome wooden, compartmented room dividers. Look them over—see what your place can accommodate, and where. Wines make for fascinating décor and are certainly conversation pieces, so why not have some on view?

Here's another hint: if he's willing, and most are, ask your wine man to keep your cases for you. He's got the right conditions in his store or warehouse. Most of them are glad to do it for case lot buyers. Besides, you save money by buying case lots. You draw on your reserves when you need a few bottles, and the rest is kept properly in between, maturing and improving all the time.

Two Wines

If you're having a rather elaborate meal, with perhaps a fish and a meat course, or if you really want to put on a bit of "side," as they say, you may want to serve more than one wine. Very well—again simplicity does it. The white precedes the red just as, in most households, a fish would come before the meat. Should your two wines be of the same color, the rule of thumb is the younger before the older. If one is sweet and one dry, let the dry precede the sweet. That's all there is to that.

Serving Temperature

This is another scary topic to many. No need to be. It's like this; red wines—the temperature of your room, achieved by bringing the wines into the room where they're going to be served the morning of the dinner, and leaving them there—standing upright, incidentally. It is quite true that "room temperature" today isn't what it used to be. If your steam-heated "room temperature" is very high, try to turn down the thermostat or stand the wine in the coolest place until dinner-time. White wines—put them in the refrig the morning of the affair, or two or three hours before dinnertime. And that goes for pink wines, the Rosés, as well. Nothing dire will happen if you leave bottles in the refrig for days. Try to avoid too much alternate cooling, warming, cooling, warming. It's the *changing* that hurts.

Above all—*never* try to warm a red by heating it, and *never* cool a white wine so long, or get it so frigid, that, when served, you can hardly distinguish it from lemon squash.

Open Reds Ahead

Open your *red* wines—pull the corks, that is, and leave them out—at least an hour before they're to be served . . . longer, if possible. This is called allowing the wine to "breathe." It makes an incredible difference, this little pre-service aeration. It doesn't hurt whites, either.

Decanting

This is another moot question, this matter of pouring the wine from bottle into decanter to avoid dregs. We drink our wines younger these days. There isn't as much deposit thrown as in Grandpa's time. There is seldom a real need to decant. Yet the British are great for decanting almost all reds (it does aerate the wine beautifully, sludge or no). The French "can't be bothered." They just pour carefully. So again, suit yourself. If you have nice decanters—decant. Simply pour the wine carefully until it shows up cloudy. Then stop and discard the rest. But do keep the cork to show, and display the empty bottles.

Napkins

For heaven's sake—no napkins wrapped around the bottle. If you're ashamed of what you're serving, don't serve it! The white wines won't be warmed by the server's hand, no matter what they say. It's just a nice-Nellyism and an affectation that's come down to us for no real reason. It's nice to know what wine you're drinking, and many hosts make a practice of not only showing, but announcing it.

In the Restaurant

Order your red wine just as soon as you can, once you've decided on your food, and have the man open it, while you munch your celery or drink your soup. White wines don't need this oxygen treatment for some reason. They just need to be nicely chilled, so also order these promptly in the restaurant so they can be in the ice bucket as long as possible. These days, most whites are precooled in the restaurant's refrigerator, ready to serve.

Store and Sommelier

A good wine—by that I mean any sound, honest wine and not just an expensive one—costs about the same no matter where it is bought in this country. Then why not patronize a wine and liquor store where wines are *important*—not where, as at some neighborhood liquor stores, they are just an "also ran"? Very often the proprietor knows less about wine than you, so he doesn't stock much of it and doesn't push it. The proprietor of a worthy establishment can, and will, become your mentor until you feel a reasonable competence—and that's

just as true of a decent and reliable sommelier (the wine waiter) in a good restaurant.

The Wine Tasting

A very popular, relatively new form of entertaining is the "Wine Tasting." This can range all the way from the most elaborate club or hotel affair, featuring dozens of wines, forests of glasses, acres of platters, scads of adjectives—to a quiet, home-testing of a few wines, perhaps with one glass for each guest, a big bowl of water for rinsing, and a tray of cubed American cheese and/or French bread to munch in between and to clean the palate.

I would say the things to guard against would be *too many* wines, *unrelated* wines, and *drinking* instead of *tasting* a lot of wines. After the reasonably experienced wine amateur has had upward of eight or nine wines, his palate is likely to have lost its cunning.

There is not much point in having a comparative tasting between a series of Rhenish wines and some reds of Burgundy. What is proved? It's the old story of comparing horses and cows. It is often fun to try Châteaux bottlings against regional Clarets —or Estate Burgundies against one another or township wines —or American wines against their European counterparts made from the same grape.

The pros in a winery spit wines on the floor after a sip, a suck, and a savor. This is not generally practicable nor desirable in an apartment! Again, use cheese or bread—not fancy provender— as palate changers!

Fill the glasses only a little bit at a tasting. Too much wine never sharpened anyone's taste buds.

The Wine Picnic

Another upcoming way to use wines is the so-called "Wine Picnic" or alfresco affair. Sharp eyes last year at the Yale Bowl would have discerned a number of tail gate parties featuring wines of one sort or another, in place of the proverbial jugs of martinis. Sausages of all kinds, cold cuts, cold chicken, cold steak—all go with a good bottle in the outdoors. Cheese and wine is the greatest gastronomic marriage in the realm.

Wine Cookery

This is a "vasty subject," as Trollope might say. Books have been written on it. Look into wine cookery, in one form or another, to one degree or another. The reasons are simple. Wine, being composed mostly of water, provides the liquid you need for many dishes *plus* subtle flavors that blend beautifully with meats, fish, whatever you are cooking. Many a French chef and housewife believe water is the death of good cookery; they use stock or soup or wine, which enrichen and flavor as they moisturize. Incidentally, the alcohol in wine or spirits cooks away, leaving the "esters" and other flavor elements, behind— so use good wine, not any old wine to ensure good flavor. Use the wine you're going to drink—that's the best way.

Wine for Health

I would not dare to discuss this serious subject in any definitive way. That would be a presumption. However, there is a vast library of works praising wine to the skies for its medicinal properties. Ask *your* doctor. Like as not, he's a member of some wine society! A glass before retiring is the best soporific you can take, and everyone knows the value of wine for the elderly.

In Europe, children begin drinking wine about the time they're weaned. They look pretty healthy in the wine-drinking countries where I've been, and certainly wine's chemistry would win more medical plaudits than would that of some other drinks for the young I know.

"L'ENBOIRE"

There is more, much more, to say about wine, but this book started out to be just a primer, and a primer it is! Once the wine virus gets into the veins, there is no cure. You will go on experimenting, reading, learning, tasting, talking. At least I think you will because that has been my experience, and the experience of the ages—ever since the first grape was squeezed by the first man and mysteriously fermented into wine in his goatskin bag! It would seem so because wine has been celebrated by every civilization in recorded history.

Probably the Babylonians first produced wine and the Phoenicians brought it to Europe. Both the Old and the New Testaments of the Bible are replete with references to wine. Even Leif the Lucky and his Vikings, discovering the wild grapes growing along the coast of North America, dubbed the unknown land Vineland, while Columbus was still sipping Rioja in Spain and Verrazano was sipping Chianti in Italy.

The tributes to wine are many, and in keeping with a terse book, here are a few terse adages to illumine my poor pun "L'En*boire*":

"Drink wine and let the water go to the mill"—Italian
"Thirst comes with drinking, when the wine is good"—French
"Bronze is the mirror of the form, wine of the heart"—Greek
"Wine is to make men happy, not to make them drunk"—
Hebrew

And finally, to a gentleman named J. H. Voss, about whom I know absolutely nothing, we owe this famous two hundred-year-old couplet:

> Who loves not woman, wine and song—
> Remains a fool his whole life long.

On this joyous counsel it seems fitting to say Hail and—

Santé!

PRONUNCIATION
of Some of
the More Common
Wine Terms

Red Wines

Name	Pronunciation
Aloxe-Corton	AH-lohss-KOHR-tohn
Bardolino (Italian)	Bar-doh-LEE-noh
Beaujolais	BOH-jo-lay
Bordeaux	BOHR-doh
Bonnes Mares	Bohn-Mahr
Cabernet Sauvignon	Cah-behr-NAY-Sah-veen-YOHN
Chambertin	SHAHM-beyr-tahn
Chambolle-Musigny	SHAHM-bohl-MOO-seen-yee
Châteauneuf-du-Pape	SHAH-toh-NUF-due-Pahp
Château Ausone	SHAH-toh-Oh-zone
Château Calon-Ségur	SHAH-toh-KAH-lohn-SAY-gure

67

Château Cheval-Blanc	SHAH-toh-SHE-vahl-Blahn
Château Gruaud-Larose	SHAH-toh-GREW-oh-Lah-ROHZ
Château Haut-Brion	SHAH-toh-Oh-Bree-OHN
Château Lafite	SHAH-toh-Lah-FEET
Château Latour	SHAH-toh-Lah-TOOR
Château Léoville-Poyferré	SHAH-toh-LAY-oh-veel-PWAH-feh-RAY
Château Margaux	SHAH-toh-MAHR-goh
Château Mouton Rothschild	SHAH-toh-Moo-tohn-ROWT-scheel
Château Pétrus	SHAH-toh-PAY-trews
Château Talbot	SHAH-toh-TAHL-boh
Côte Rôtie	Koht-Roh-TEE
cru	krew
Gévrey-Chambertin	JEH-vray-SHAHM-behr-tahn
Hermitage	AIR-mee-tahj
La Tâche	Lah-TASH
maderisé	mah-deh-ree-ZAY
Médoc	May-dock
Moulin-à-Vent	MOO-lahn-ah-Vahn
Musigny	MEU-seen-yee
Pinot Noir	Pee-noh-NWAHR
Pommard	Poh-mahr
Richebourg	REE-she-boor
Rioja (Spanish)	Ree-OH-ha
Romanée-Conti	Roh-mah-NAY-Kahn-TEE
St. Émilion	Sahnt-Ay-mee-lee-OHN
St. Estèphe	Sahnt-Ay-STEHF
St. Julien	Sahnt-Joo-ly-EHN
sec	seck

| Valpolicella (Italian) | Vahl-pohl-ee-CHEH-lah |
| Volnay | VOHL-nay |

Rosé
(Roh-Zay')

Name	*Pronunciation*
Grenache Rosé	Gre-NASH-Roh-ZAY
Tavel	Tah-vehl

White Wines
(including a few German terms)

Auslese (German)	OWS-lay-seh
Barsac	BAHR-sahk
blanc	blahn
Bernkasteler (German)	BEHRN-kahst-ler
brut	breu
Chablis	SHAH-blee
Château d'Yquem	SHAH-toh-DEE-kem
Chenin Blanc	She-nahn-BLAHN
Corton-Charlemagne	Kohr-ton-SHAHR-leh-mahn-yeh
Graves	Grahv
Hermitage Blanc	AIR-mee-tahj Blahn
Le Montrachet	Luh-MOHN-rah-shay
Liebfraumilch (German)	LEEB-frow-milsh
Meursault	MIHR-soh
Moselle (German)	Mo-zel
Pinot Blanc	PEE-noh Blahn
Pinot Chardonnay	PEE-noh Shar-doh-nay
Pouilly-Fuissé	Pwee-yee-Feee-SAY

Pouilly-Fumé	Pwee-yee-Feu-MAY
Riesling (German)	Rees-ling
Sancerre	Sahn-sair
Sauternes	Sow-TEHRN
Sauvignon	Soh-vee-YOHN
Schloss Vollrads (German)	Shloss FALL-rods
Semillon	Seh-mee-YOHN
Spätlese (German)	SPAYT-lay-zeh
Sylvaner	SEEL-vah-ner
Tokay (Hungarian)	Toh-kay
Traminer	Trah-MEE-ner
Verdicchio (Italian)	Vair-DEEK-yoh
Vouvray	Voo-vray

VINTAGE CHART

Use this chart as a rule of thumb only. Do not be a slave to it.

	1952	1953	1954	1955	1956	1957
Burgundy—Red	10	9	5	10	5	8
Burgundy—White	9	10	4	9	4	8
Bordeaux—Red	10	9	4	9	5	8
Bordeaux—White	9	10	5	9	4	8
Rhône	10	10	6	9	6	9
Rhine & Moselle	7	8	3	7	3	8
Alsace	7	8	5	8	4	8
Champagne	10	9	nv	8	nv	8

Above chart is to be read from 0 to 10, in which 10 is finest and 0 is zero. nv means "no vintage"; poor. It is well to keep in mind that the experts often change their opinions in midstream, as time goes on. Remember too, most normal whites, of 1960 or before, are getting old now.

There is good wine made in off years. Seek it out for value.

1958	1959*	1960	1961	1962	1963	1964†
6	10	5	10	8	6	9
8	10	6	10	8	8	8
6	10	6	10	8	6	8
6	10	4	10	9	5	9 (Dry) 5 (Sweet)
7	10	4	9	9	5	7
8	9	4	10	8	8	8 (Rhine) 9 (Moselle)
7	10	5	10	8	7	9
nv	8	nv	10	9	6	9

* The '59s are no longer the "wines of the century."
† The '64s are still young. It would appear now as a generally great year but with a few reservations.

1965 bodes fair to being another European "selective" year—some good, some bad, *most poor*. California's crop—large, and in the main very good; New York wines—OK.

1958	1959*	1960	1961	1962	1963	1964†	
6	10	5	10	8	6	9	
8	10	6	10	6	8	8	
6	10	6	10	8	6	8	
6	10	4	10	6	3	9	(Dry)
						9	(Sweet)
7	10	4	6	6	5	7	
8	6	4	10	8	8	8	(Rhine)
						9	(Moselle)
7	10	5	8	8	7	9	
nv	8	6	10	9	6	9	

* The '59s are no longer the "wines of the century".
† The '64s are still young. It would appear now as a generally great year but with a few reservations.
1965 bodes fair to being another European "selective" year—some good, some bad, most poor. California's crop—large, and in the main very good; New York wines—OK.

73

SUGGESTIONS
IN CHART FORM
for Matching Wines
to Foods

Red Wines

ALL RED MEATS including *Roasts, Steaks, Stews; Game, Duck, Goose; Veal* and *Cheese* (White Wine and Rosé also acceptable)

BURGUNDY

$6. TO $15.

Richebourg
Musigny
Le Chambertin
Clos de Vougeot
La Tâche
Bonnes Mares

Les Grands Echézeaux
Romanée-Conti
is so expensive, and so
seldom encountered,
it seems almost foolish
to include it.

$3.50 TO $6.

Vosne-Romanée
Aloxe-Corton
Gévrey-Chambertin

Pommard
Nuits-Saint-Georges
Beaune

$1.75 TO $3.

Mercurey   *Fixin*

Beaujolais

Try the named ones—

Brouilly
Morgon
Juliénas

Moulin-à-Vent
Fleurie

Red Wines

ALL RED MEATS including *Roasts, Steaks, Stews; Game, Duck, Goose; Veal* and *Cheese* (White Wine and Rosé also acceptable)

BORDEAUX (CLARET)

Château Wines

$5. TO $12.

1st Growths

Château Lafite	*Château Haut-Brion*
Château Latour	*Château Ausone*
Château Margaux	*Château Cheval Blanc*
Château Mouton Rothschild	*Château Pétrus*

$3. TO $6.50

2nd Growths

There are many. These are only a few.

Château Gruaud-Larose	*Château Pichon-Longueville*
Château Canon	*Château Montrose*
Château Léoville-Poyferré	*Château Lascombes*

$2.50 TO $4.

3rd to 5th Grades

There are many. These are only a few.

Château Palmer	*Château Talbot*
Château Meyney	*Château Pontet-Canet*
Château Calon-Ségur	*Château Prieuré-Lichine*
Château Beycheville	*Château Lynch-Bages*

Regional Wines

$1.75 TO $2.50

Saint Émilion	*Margaux*
Saint Julien	*Pomerol*
Saint Estèphe	and others

Red Wines

ALL RED MEATS including *Roasts, Steaks, Stews; Game, Duck, Goose; Veal* and *Cheese* (White Wine and Rosé also acceptable)

RHÔNE

$2. TO $4.

Châteauneuf-du-Pape
Côte Rôtie
Hermitage

SPANISH

$1.75 TO $2.25

Rioja

PORTUGUESE

$1.25 TO $2.25

Dão Tinto
Colares
Vinhas Tinto

HUNGARIAN

$2. TO $3.50

Egri Bikavér (Bull's Blood)
Kadarka

SWISS

$2. TO $3.

Dôle

ITALIAN

$1.50 TO $2.50

Chianti
Valpolicella
Bardolino
Barbera
Barolo
Gattinara

YUGOSLAVIAN

$1. TO $2.

Dingac
Blatina
Merlot

GREEK

$1.25 TO $2.25

Naoussa
Kokineli

TURKISH

$1.50 TO $2.50

Trakya
Buzbag

Red Wines

ALL RED MEATS including *Roasts, Steaks, Stews; Game, Duck, Goose; Veal* and *Cheese* (White Wine and Rosé also acceptable)

AMERICAN

California

UP TO $3.00

Pinot Noir—from the red Burgundy grape
Cabernet Sauvignon—from the red Bordeaux grape
Zinfandel—light, pleasant (no European counterpart)
Gamay—from the Beaujolais grape

Some to look for: Almadén, Martini, Krug, Masson, Cresta Blanca, Korbel, Beaulieu, Concannon, Buena Vista, Inglenook, Berenger, Sebastiani, Wente, Martin Ray, Christian Brothers, Asti, Mayacamas, Assumption Abbey, Mirassou, Maitre D', 11 Cellars, Ambassador, Ficklin (port); Gallo, Roma, Guild, Italian Swiss, Petri, Cucamonga, East Side, Heitz, Regina, etc., are producers of generic and popular wines, many under trade marks and trade names of their own.

Eastern

$1.25 TO $2.25

Various types made from native grapes and their hybrids, under various names. Seek out: New York: Widmer, Taylor, Great Western, Gold Seal; Meier's of Ohio.

White Wines

Fish, Shellfish, Poultry, Chicken, Turkey (Red Wine also acceptable), *Ham, Veal* (light Red Wine also acceptable)

BURGUNDY

$3.50 TO $10.

Le Montrachet
is the greatest—
scarce, expensive.
Bâtard-Montrachet
Chassagne-Montrachet

Chevalier-Montrachet
Corton-Charlemagne
Meursault
Corton Blanc

$2.50 TO $5.

Pouilly-Fuissé

covers a multitude of
wines—good and bad.

Chablis

Seek out hyphenated
ones such as
Chablis-Vaudésir
Chablis-Valmur

Look for such French shippers as Jadot, Drouhin, Latour, Ropiteau, Laguiche, Moreau, Leflaive, Chanson, Chauvenet, Calvert, B & G, or for such importers as Frederick Wildman, Browne-Vintners, Dreyfus-Ashby, Kobrand, Wile, Schieffelin (Sichel), House of Burgundy, Leeds, Carillon, Austin Nichols.

LOIRE

$1.75 TO $4.

Muscadet—dry, inexpensive
Sancerre

Pouilly-Fumé
Vouvray

White Wines

Fish, Shellfish, Poultry, Chicken, Turkey (Red Wine also acceptable), *Ham, Veal* (light Red Wine also acceptable)

BORDEAUX
Sweet

$3.50 TO $10.

Château d'Yquem
is the queen of the
Sauternes—always scarce,
always sweet, always expensive.
Price depends on vintage.

$2.50 TO $5.

Château Climens
Château Filhot
Château de Suduiraut
Château Rayne-Vigneau

Dry
$2. TO $5.

Château Haut-Brion Blanc
Château Carbonnieux

Château Olivier

There are also wines simply labeled Graves, Sauternes, Haut-Sauternes, Barsac. These are regional wines and will cost less than the Châteaux; from $2. to $3.

RHÔNE
$2.00 TO $3.50

Hermitage Blanc
—Chante Alouette
La Chapelle

Also, Arbois and
Provençal wines
are worth trying.

81

White Wines

Fish, Shellfish, Poultry, Chicken, Turkey (Red Wine also acceptable), *Ham, Veal* (light Red Wine also acceptable)

ALSATIAN
$1.75 TO $3.75

Riesling   *Traminer*
Sylvaner   *Gewürtztraminer*
Lorentz, Hugel, Willm, Dopff are good shippers.

GERMAN
Rhine Wines

in brown bottles
$2.50 TO $6.

Schloss Vollrads
Schloss Johannesberg
Marcobrunner
Rüdesheimer—
and hundreds of
others.

When marked *Spätlese, Beerenauslese, Trockenbeerenauslese,* prices can run up to $50! These rare wines are likely to be sweet and are best for dessert.

Moselle Wines

in green bottles
$3. TO $6.

Berncasteler Doktor
is the king here—
scarce, expensive.
Graacher Himmelreich
Piesporter Goldtröpfchen

Wehlener Sonnenuhr
Maximin Grunhauser
For special bottlings, prices can go skyward, as in the Rhines.

White Wines

Fish, Shellfish, Poultry, Chicken, Turkey (Red Wine also acceptable), *Ham, Veal* (light Red Wine also acceptable)

ITALIAN
$1.50 TO 3.50

Orvieto
Verdicchio
Soave
White Chianti

AUSTRIAN
$2. TO $4.

Gumpoldskirchner—semi-sweet
Loibner Kaiserwein—dry
Kremser
Nussberger

GREEK
$1.50 TO $2.50

Pallini
St. Helena
Cave Minos

SPANISH
$1.50 TO 2.25

Rioja (White)
Montilla

SWISS
$1.75 TO $2.75

Neuchâtel
Fendant
Dézalay

HUNGARIAN
$2. TO $.5

Tokay Aszu—sweet
Tokay Szamorodni—drier
Other table wines:
Badacsonyi
Gyöngyosi (sparkling)

YUGOSLAVIAN
$1. TO $2.

Zilavka
Rizling
Chipon White

PORTUGUESE
$1.50 TO $2.50.

Vinhas Branco
Vinho Verde Branco

White Wines

Fish, Shellfish, Poultry, Chicken, Turkey (Red Wine also acceptable), *Ham, Veal* (light Red Wine also acceptable)

CHILEAN
$1.50 TO $2.

In Bocksbeutel
(squatty, flask bottles)
Undurraga is a good one

TURKISH
$1.50 TO $2.50

Kulüp Sarabi
Trakya

SOUTH AFRICAN
$1.50 TO $2.50.

Constantia

AUSTRALIAN
$1.50 TO $2.

Yolumba

AMERICAN
UP TO $3.50.

Pinot Chardonnay and *Pinot Blanc*—counterparts of French
White Burgundy
Semillon, Sauvignon—counterparts of French White Bordeaux
Chenin Blanc—counterpart of French Vouvray
Riesling, Grey Riesling, Traminer, Gewürtztraminer, Sylvaner
—counterparts of German and Alsatian Wines
Green Hungarian—exclusive to America

Masson's *Emerald Dry,* from a new Riesling hybrid, is very popular. Also
such "generics" as California Chablis, Sauterne, Rhine, etc., and Eastern
wines: Niagara, Diamond, Delaware, and Scuppernong, etc. See list of
producers under Red Wines, American.

Champagnes

Champagne goes with anything at any time

FRENCH
VINTAGE—$6.50 TO $15.50
NON-VINTAGE—$5.50 TO $8.50

Moët & Chandon (Cuvée Dom Pérignon is their top), Krug, Mumm, Piper-Heidsieck, Charles Heidsieck, Roederer, Taittinger (blanc de blancs—all white grapes), Bollinger, Perrier-Jouët, Irroy, Laurent-Perrier, Pommery & Greno, Mercier, Ayala, Veuve Clicquot, Lanson, Ruinart

AMERICAN
California
$3.50 TO $7.50

Korbel (Natur even drier than their Brut), Almadén, Weibel, Kornell, Masson, Beaulieu's B/V, Cresta Blanca, and others (Charmat process: Christian Brothers, Gallo, Léjon, Guild, Italian Swiss, Roma, Maitre D').

Eastern
$4. TO $6.50

Taylor, Great Western, Gold Seal, Charles Fournier

GERMAN
$3. TO $5.
Sekt

ITALY
$3. TO $5.
Asti Spumante

Rosé Wines

Salmon, Fish Stews, some *Casseroles, Steak* on a summer's day, some rich *Cheeses, Omelettes* or *Soufflés, Cold Cuts*

$2. TO $3.50

Tavel (Rhône), the best, and best known. Other popular Rosés from *Anjou, Loire, Alsace, Provence.* U.S.A. offers good Rosés $1.50 to $2. *Grenache Rosé* of Almadén and Wente's *Livermore Rosé* are very popular, as is Gallo's Rosé. Italy's Rosés of Lake Garda, very good. Also, *Lancers* and *Mateus* from Portugal.

Dessert Wines

Fruit, Compotes, rich *Cakes* or *Tarts,* some dessert *Cheeses*

Here is where your great *Sauternes* come in, also the sweet *Barsacs;* the "special" German *Auslese* dessert wines made of overripe grapes; *Port, Marsala, Angelica,* sweet *Sherries,* sweet *Tokay,* sweet *Madeira (Boal or Malmsey),* Italy's *Est Est Est,* Greece's *Mavrodaphne, Asti Spumante* of Italy, and Germany's *Sekt* and France's sweet *doux* and *sec* Champagnes.

After Dinner

Port (the various types).
Cognac — a brandy distilled from grapes grown in the demarcated area of the Charente, around the cities of Cognac and Jarnac. (All other distilled grape wine is *Brandy* — not *Cognac*.)
Armagnac is from the demarcated area in the department of Gers.
Calvados — from apples (Normandy).
Marc — from pits and hulls of the grapes, distilled and aged — called *Grappa* in Italy.

LIQUEURS

Some distilled, some infusions, some secret formulae, some fruit (white) alcohols such as *Kirsch, Framboise, Poire, Mirabelle*. There are hundreds of kinds, types and brands, too numerous to record. A few: *Cointreau, Strega, Bénédictine, Chartreuse* (green and yellow), *Galliano, Crème de Menthe, Drambuie, Grand Marnier*, ad infinitum! *Pernod, Berger*, and *Ricard* are licorice-flavored, usually served as apéritifs.

YOUR
CELLAR

Wine	Quantity	When Purchased	Cost

Supplier & Comments

Wine	Quantity	When Purchased	Cost

Supplier & Comments

INDEX

96

97